Stations of the Cross
A Weapon of Warfare

*The sword for overcoming
the powers of darkness
afflicting your life*
(Colossians 2:15; Revelation 1:16-20; 19:15, 20 -21)

In order to enjoy the fullness of Life in God (John 10:10)

Sir Charles Muoka Ph.D

Stations of the Cross: A Weapon of Warfare

By

Sir Charles Muoka Ph.D

Nihil Obstat

Very Rev. Msgr. Anthony Anijielo
Censor Librorum, Enugu

Imprimatur

✠ Calistus V. C. Onaga
BISHOP OF ENUGU
(December 05, 2021)

Copyright © 2014 Sir Charles Muoka
Third Edition 2017
Second Edition 2016
First Published in 2014
All rights reserved.
Without limiting the rights under copyright reserved above, no part of this publication maybe used or reproduced in any manner whatsoever without written permission of the copyright owner or the publisher.

National Library of Nigeria Cataloguing-in-Publication Data
   MUOKA, Charles Chuwkugozie, 1964 —
     Stations of the Cross: A Weapon of Warfare
       1. Stations of the Cross. 2. Catholic Church -Prayers and devotions
     I. Title.
     BX2040.M971   2017   264.0274
     ISBN: 978-978-961-824-8   (pbk)   AACR2

Published in the Federal Republic of Nigeria by

 COMMUNICATIONS LIMITED

For more information and bulk orders, please contact:
Marketing Department, CMM Communications Limited
Muoka Plaza, 18 Obinagu Road, Abakpa-Nike, P.O. Box 1139, Enugu, Nigeria
Telephone: 0803-360-0825   Email: cmmcommunicationsltd@yahoo.com

> The author wishes to hear from you. Please do be kind to share your testimonies, questions and comments with him by email to cmcmuoka@yahoo.com. He can also be reached for counseling, prayers, seminars and conferences.

Credits:
www.catholic.org: Stations of the Cross Format
Upper Room Ministries: www.frnjokufoundation.org: Emmanuel Town, Ugwuomu, Emene, Enugu, Nigeria: Exclusive right of the use of the images of the Stations of the Cross Worldwide.

The Holy Spirit and Cross of Jesus whose powers have overcome for me the twenty - three years of ferocious siege by the enemy upon my life. Now, I can laugh and fly for God has made me a spectacle among men – having erased the shame and defeats of my life (Isa. 60:1-3; Phil 2:15).

To my family, especially the love of my life, Nkechi Elizabeth and our adorable son Charles Chukwugozie Michael Jr., my glory. Thanks go to the rest of my family for bearing with me in the wilderness in great lack, rejections, pains, mockery, and dishonor, with patient endurance and even often times without clear understanding of everything, yet bearing love. Life would have been a misery without your love, care, understanding, encouragement and honour.

To the Christian pilgrim, I encourage you to be steadfast, for the battle is not yours but the Lord's. Your duty, as a demonstration of your radical faith in God is to sincerely commit to living a life of radical obedience to God's commands – and, then, pronounce the words in invocation as laid out for you in this book. And then stand still to see the salvation of the Lord in awesome measures in your life as the enemies of your life are overcome (Exod. 14:13).

To the enemies of my life, I thank you for every stone and obstacle put in the path of my life and destiny, for indeed they were truly what I needed to have found my- self. Every experience I have had in the past twenty - three years has immeasurably shaped and sharpened my life, and now, for me, having found Christ, life has a far greater meaning. As you can see, I am fulfilling my destiny and winning friends for God (2Cor. 5:20). This prayer book bears true witness to that fulfilment. Thank you for your help, the experiences and the lessons learned. For those bickering, do not worry. I forgive you for every offence against me and hope you forgive mine. But if you continue to remain an enemy of Christ, you certainly will remain my enemy. So now, the choice is yours.

Contents

Foreword	v
Preface	vi
Acknowledgment	viii
Ten Pathways for Effective Warfare	ix

Introduction: Prayer at the Altar 1

Stations

One	Jesus Is Condemned to Death	2
Two	Jesus Carries the Cross	6
Three	Jesus Falls For the First Time	10
Four	Jesus Beholds His Holy Mother	14
Five	Simon Helps Jesus Carry His Cross	18
Six	Veronica Wipes the Face of Jesus	22
Seven	Jesus Falls the Second Time	26
Eight	Women of Jerusalem Mourn for Jesus	30
Nine	Jesus Falls For the Third Time	34
Ten	Jesus Is Stripped of His Garments	38
Eleven	Jesus Is Nailed to the Cross	42
Twelve	Jesus Dies on the Cross	46
Thirteen	Jesus Is Taken Down from the Cross	50
Fourteen	Jesus Is Laid in the Tomb	54
Conclusion:	Intentions of the Holy Father the Pope and Closing Prayer	58

Foreword

The purpose of the practice of the devotion of the Stations of the Cross is to make us contemplate the sufferings of Christ that presaged our salvation. But, more importantly, this practice is to relate the importance of the sufferings of Christ to our own lives. Like Him, we can, in spite of the multifarious challenges and crosses that well-up in our personal lives, surge ahead in the full realisation that the Father never abandons us. He is always with us.

The cross is ever present in our lives in this physical order. This notwithstanding, we must never give up but always see the light at the end of the tunnel. The enemy, the evil one, can never vanquish us. Let us never play into his hands by turning our back to God when we are immersed in darkness. At Christ's own darkest moment His resolute response was: "Father into your hands I commit my spirit" (Luke 23:46). And this led to His final victory. Similarly, if we refuse to give up - if we refuse to deny God when the storms of life assail us - we shall equally emerge superbly victorious.

The various stations in the Stations of the Cross reflect the different trials that assail us in life; when friends and antagonists sell us out, we can think of the betrayal of Christ and draw the strength to forge ahead. When we encounter repeated failures in business, we can compare them to Christ's several falls under the weight of the cross and learn from Him to never give up.

This booklet may help those who labour and are overburdened to approach Christ and to learn from His own personal experience that intimacy with Him does not mean absolute security and shielding against the challenges of life. The underlying lesson in this booklet is that if we share in the cross of Christ by our own trials we can confidently look forward to sharing the glories of life with Him – both here and ultimately hereafter.

Very Reverend Monsignor Dr. Anthony Anijielo

Preface

Why I wrote this version of the Passion of Jesus

This is in response to Jesus's divine call in Matthew 11:12 that the kingdom of God suffers violence, and the violent take it by force. The epistle of Paul in Ephesians 6:12 clarified that we do not battle against flesh and blood, but with principalities, powers, and authorities in the heavenly world.

It then becomes evident that the battle is not ordinary – not physical warfare but spiritual. This presupposes that the weapon for defence, attack and counter attack has to be at the same realm of the spirit. Victory in the spirit bears manifestation in the physical world.

Fortunately, in the core of the spiritual warfare, Jesus the conqueror has won the battle for the children of God through His victory on the cross (Eph. 1:7; Col. 2:14-15). And your union with Him in baptism appropriates for you this victory (Rom. 6: 3-5). Therefore, it is your free right to possess and enjoy the fullness of the treasures in the kingdom of God (John 10:10).

However, the enemy is resilient and so tries to deny you this right (Dan.10:11-14) through temptations, our fallen human nature and the world (James 1:12-15; Rom. 7:14-24; James 4:1-5); hence Jesus's call for violent warfare (i.e., radical faith shown through life of radical obedience to God's commands), the one sure strategy of overcoming the enemy to retain your possession (James 4:7, 10; Rom. 8:1-17). It is an unfailing weapon for the accused, pursued, tormented, opposed, oppressed, barren, weak, neglected, caged, hurt, sorrowful, frightened, defeated, confused, humiliated, isolated, denied, rejected, hated, resented, mocked, traumatised, and the like and yet those who are hopeful; and those with great love and passion for God, which will allow them to rise in boldness to confront the enemy (Eph. 6:12).

Now, in that resilient status, to take possession of the treasure (Eph. 1:3), all you need to do as a pilgrim is to show evidence of your sonship in God as your gate-pass (your radical faith in God demonstrated through your life of radical obedience to His commands). Then, raise the cross of Jesus Christ - the sword for overcoming the enemy (Col. 2:15; Rev. 1:4-19, 19:15) and forcefully take possession of the treasures that are truly yours in Christ Jesus (John 10:10). The sonship evidence pass and the cross, automatically open unto the pilgrim the invincible force of God for the defeat of the enemy (1 John 5:1-5). Any pilgrim having challenges with the sonship pass due to sin, can simply reconcile with God, and then, once again present the pass for an entry to the treasure (1 John 1:8-10).

This prayer book reveals the power of your sonship authority in God through the passion of Jesus (Rom. 6: 3-4) as well as sacred methods of raising the cross of Jesus as weapons for both defence and counter attack (1Tim. 1:18) against the enemies of your life, in order to easily overcome them and win your desired victory in God. In this way, you may enjoy the fullness of the treasures of the kingdom of God that are truly yours (John 10:10).

This secret is what is absent in all other versions of the passion of Jesus Christ. So this is an uncommon prayer book for spiritual warfare - hence it's title.

In your hand, you hold a divine weapon for overcoming the ferocious enemies of your life. However, remember that a weapon that is not utilised is as useless as money in the bank that is not accessed while the owner suffers hunger and poverty. Therefore, act in confidence, trusting God, for He is awaiting your move of faith in Him.
Congratulations!

Acknowledgements

The following made this work possible and I hold in highest esteem their immeasurable contributions to my Christian life and this book:

The Holy Spirit inspires me, especially in this book, and teaches and guides me on all knowledge. He reveals Christ and all truths, and particularly, those of the stations of the cross, to me. Without this guidance, the book would have been impossible, as I would have lacked the knowledge, understanding and inspiration for the work.

Rev. Fr. Dr. Uche Stephen Njoku is an erudite teacher and mentor from whom I learned the art of the teaching ministry in God's kingdom. His ministry the Upper Room was a truly nurturing ground for my early new Christian life.

Very Rev. Monsignor Dr. Anthony Anijielo is my mentor extraordinaire, whose trust and favour offered me the opportunity of my life – the Christ Ambassadors – a Catholic fellowship group with the vision of building up Catholics who are Spirit-filled, vibrant, and knowledgeable, and who have wisdom and deep rooted faith in Christ. Their mission is to use the vehicle of God's Word to build up Catholics whose lives are true testimonies of God's power in action as a means of winning friends for Him.

In this platform of lay Christians, as its pioneer founding president, my teaching gifts and charisma are being revealed and nurtured. All thanks to the support and encouragement of Monsignor Anijielo.

The Christ Ambassadors Fellowship Group are my most beloved brethren, whose love, support, cooperation and honour elevated me beyond what I am. I celebrate the power of God within us.

Rev. Fr. Dan Ileka is a dear friend and a fearless warrior, who enthroned the presence of Jesus Christ-the general of the Lord's army (Rev.19:14), through the Blessed Sacrament into the enemy's encampment in one of our family's encounters, and then followed Him, with us trailing behind. Then His divine presence smashed and uprooted all strongholds, freeing all captives.

Ten Pathways for Effective Warfare

These pathways are like refiners – to prepare you spiritually for a successful warfare programme (Mal. 3:3-4; 1King 6:7).

1. Make it a forty – day warfare prayer programme.
2. At the beginning set clearly your intentions for the warfare.
3. Attend mass daily and ensure to receive communion.
4. Go to confession at least two times (at the beginning and end of the programme).
5. Fast for the forty days and choose periods of some discomfort.
6. Give donation to an orphanage around you, or respond to someone in need who may have been asking for your help as a demonstration of your love and compassion for your neighbor. Speak and make clear your intentions for the alms (as your seed offering of faith to God).
7. Forgive every offence against you, and be at peace with all.
8. Run away from sin especially the sin of the flesh.
9. Decide on a life covenant with God - a vow you are sure to keep all the days of your life and that must be a sacrifice – one that will cost you something, in order to provoke His attention, mercy, and favour towards you.
10. Commit to a life of radical - deep-seated obedience to God's commands for the rest of your life.

Note: *Choose to remain in battle until you obtain answer(s) to your petition(s) from God and for its retention.*

Introduction

The Stations of the Cross
(Col. 2:15; 1 Tim.1: 18)

Prayer at the Altar

Kneel, do the sign of the cross and say Gloria Patri:
In the name of the Father, and of the Son, and of the Holy Spirit, as it was in the beginning, is now, and ever shall be, world without end. Amen!

Confess your sins to the Lord and then say the Act of Contrition:

O God, I am sorry and beg pardon for all my sins, and detest them above all things, because they have crucified my loving Saviour Jesus Christ, and, most of all, because they offend your infinite goodness, and I firmly resolve, by the help of your grace, never to offend you again, and to avoid the occasion of sin . Amen!

Raise your intentions/petitions unto the Lord (recount to Him what your enemies have done - or are doing to you - and what you desire from Him. But remember that vengeance is only unto the Lord.

O Lord Jesus, my Redeemer and Saviour, can my whole being ever thank you enough for your gift of redemption? For out of your deepest love and care, which is in your nature, you became the sacrificial Lamb paid as the ransom for my sins; bearing the condemnation and punishment for my failures and offences. Thus, you have redeemed me from my just punishments. Oh, what an awesome God you are! None is ever like you! Your love, Lord, surpasses all understanding!

Now, merciful Redeemer, I implore thee, to humbly permit me to share with thee in this journey of thy cross that I am about to embark upon. As I meditate on thy sufferings, they shall appropriate for me thy mercy, favour, and power, which I need to overcome the fearsome attacks of my enemies, who are stronger than I am.

Lord, I acknowledge that I am nothing without you. You are my only strength, power and wisdom, and I need you to fight this battle and to win it. Come, Lord, the Holy Spirit of Jesus to my aid! Amen!

Chapter One

First Station
Jesus Is Condemned to Death

Isaiah 53:6-8; Matthew 27:15-26; Mark 15:6-15; Luke 23:1-25; John 19:1-16

V. We adore thee, O Christ, and praise thee.
R. *Because by thy holy cross, thou hast redeemed the world.*

Meditation
Now, in the name of Jesus Christ and in the authority of this first station, summon all satanic and occult spirits (Rev. 12:12, 10:1-6, 13:1-6, 17:1-2; Ezek. 29:1-6; Isa. 27:1; Mark 5:1-13), false altars (1Cor. 10:20), shrines, temples, principalities, powers, and dominions, as well as your human accusers, pursuers and tormentors (Eph. 6:12) – all those afflicting your life - to come forth with every of their demands, accusations and judgments, rightly or unrightly, and their weapons of warfare against you, to the foot of the cross of Jesus.

Here, Jesus stands as the willing ransom – the sacrificial Lamb offered in your place to bear every of your punishment as passed in judgment over the offences of your life. Thus, this redeems you from due punishment (Isa. 53:4-7), having been condemned to die on your behalf (Isa. 53:6-8; Matt. 27:15-26; Mark 15:6-15; Luke 23:1-25; John 19:1-16), and, thereby, setting you free from every condemnation of your life (Gal. 5:1).

So, today and now, in faith in the cross of Jesus and in this station, know truly that you are a free man or woman - free from every accusation, judgment and condemnation of your life. Let the confidence of this freedom strengthen you and move you into this battle as one sufficiently prepared by the Lord to win.

Prayer

Lord Jesus, I acknowledge that I am guilty of my sins and truly deserve to bear the punishments due to me. Please forgive me out of your love and mercy. Amen! Hence, I thank you, Lord, for offering your life as a ransom for mine, thus, setting me free from all my guilt. Amen!

You spirits, powers, authorities and dominions, my accusers, pursuers, tormentors and all enemies of my life (Eph. 6:12) in the authority of the cross of Jesus Christ and this first station, Jesus having been condemned in my place and in the authority of my baptism in Him (Rom. 6:3-4), I invoke against you the mysterious power in the cross of Jesus and this station for my freedom from any further condemnation from you. In the name of Jesus Christ I decree and declare, by fire and by force, that I am free from all your condemnations, demands, obligations, and so forth upon my life, having been set free by the condemnation of Jesus Christ, the ransom for my life (Job 22:28; Matt. 18:18; Isa. 53:6-; Matt. 27:15-26; Mark 15:6-15; Luke 23:1-25; John 19:1-16 and Gal. 5:1). The cross of Jesus and this station shall, therefore, stand in perpetuity for my defence, against you, in the name of Jesus Christ. Amen!

Our Father, who art in heaven, hallowed be thy name. Thy kingdom come, thy will be done on earth, as it is in heaven. And give us this day our daily bread, and forgive us our trespasses as we forgive those who trespass against us. And lead us not into temptation, but deliver us from evil. Amen!

Hail Mary, full of grace, the Lord is with thee. Blessed art thou among women, and blessed is the Fruit of thy womb, Jesus. Holy

Mary, Mother of God, pray for us sinners, now and at the hour of our death. Amen!

Glory be to the Father, and to the Son, and to the Holy Spirit, as it was in the beginning, is now, and ever shall be, world without end. Amen!

Chapter Two

Second Station
Jesus Carries the Cross

Isaiah 53:4-6, 8; Matthew 27:31; Mark 15:15-20; Luke 23:25-26; John19:15-17

V. We adore thee, O Christ, and praise thee.
R. ***Because by thy holy cross, thou hast redeemed the world.***

Meditation
Be it known to you that it is a deception from the pit of hell for the demons, spirits, dominions, authorities, powers, false altars (1Cor. 10:20), temples, shrines, and their human agents (Eph. 6:12) to entrap your life in sorrow. The Lord's will for your life is that you should have life and have it in abundance (John 10:10). In carrying the cross, Jesus carried with Him every burden and affliction of your life, setting you free from the punishment you truly deserved for your sins, thus, making you whole (Isa. 53:4-5; John 19:16-17).

Through your baptism, you have come into a union with Christ Jesus in carrying your cross (Rom. 6:3-4). So His spirit and mysterious power fill you in joy untold - beyond human understanding, as it lessens the burden and pains of your cross and creates a mercy for you and a favour path-way to freedom from it (Matt. 11:28-30), hence, guaranteeing that your cross can never crush you as your enemies intend.

My dearest, note today, that your cross is your victory. When you invite Jesus into the challenges of your life and begin to live a life of radical obedience, God's doors of mercy and favour are automatically opened to work for you, enriching you with an out pouring of His blessings (Hos. 10:12). This is a mystery the enemy cannot understand. God uses the cross as a tool of opening us up to virgin grounds, new opportunities in order to pour out His mercy and favour upon us so His power and might could be made manifest (Hos. 10:11-12).

So when Jesus said, "carry your cross and follow me", He meant "Surrender yourself to me, lean on me and I will give you rest from your cross" (Matt. 11:28-30).

Therefore, do not fear the cross. Nor should you resent it. Rather embrace it and surrender it to the Lord. Let it become part of your motivation for righteousness that you may reap the abundant blessings of mercy and favour of God (Hos. 10:12), living life in abundance as God has purposed (John 10:10). Make the decision of surrender right now, and make it as a covenant with God. And so your cross shall become your victory.

Prayer

O Lord Jesus, what a loving God you are, offering to carry my burden even when I live in sin and; showing the depth of your love and mercy. Lord, no one can ever equal you. I, therefore, surrender my cross and myself to you, and invite you to reunite me to yourself and grant me rest from my cross.
From this day, I promise to live a life of obedience to your commands and to always strive in all things to please you. Amen! Hence, today I enter into this - special covenant- with you as my seed offering of faith for my petitions to you. (Clearly declare the covenant to which you want to enter with God, that is, the sacrifice(s) you are willing to make for the petitions you have raised unto the Lord. Or recommit yourself to your existing covenant with God if you already have one and do not wish to make a new one).

You satanic and occult spirits (Rev. 17:1-2) (mentioning any fearsome spirit in your locality), dominions, authorities, powers, false altars (1Cor. 10: 20), shrines, temples, and your human agents (Eph. 6:12), you laden my life in afflictions, untold cycles of failures and indebtedness, bareness, rejections, disappointments, humiliation, near success syndrome, the action of working like an elephant and eating like an ant, chronic delays, confusion, oppression, hatred, wickedness, betrayal, limitation, and so on. All have one intent, to ensure that my progress and future are ensnared, overburdened with unending difficulties without a chance of a sustainable growth, and a repressed destiny, a destiny unfulfilled.

But I join God in laughing at you, for you have been tricked again just like you were with the killing of Jesus. God again has shown the supremacy of His wisdom and power over you. You see, by your entrapping me, you activated the sacred mysterious power in my baptism in Christ Jesus (Rom. 6:3-4) to release to me the grace to cling unto the Lord as my last and hopeful resort in line with His Word in Matthew 11:28-30, thus causing my being showered with His spiritual blessings in the heavenly world (Eph. 1:3). Thereby, this guarantees me rest from all my tribulations from you forever (Isa. 54:11-17; Matt. 11:28-30; Heb. 3:7-19, 4:1-11).

Therefore, in the name of Jesus, I invoke the mysterious power of His cross and this station to stand for my defence in perpetuity as standards against you from any further attempt to ever burden my life again. Amen (Job 22:28; Matt. 18:18)!

Our Father, who art in heaven, hallowed be thy name. Thy kingdom come, thy will be done on earth, as it is in heaven. And give us this day our daily bread, and forgive us our trespasses as we forgive those who trespass against us. And lead us not into temptation, but deliver us from evil. Amen!

Hail Mary, full of grace, the Lord is with thee. Blessed art thou among women and blessed is the Fruit of thy womb, Jesus. Holy Mary, Mother of God, pray for us sinners, now and at the hour of our death. Amen!

Glory be to the Father, and to the Son, and to the Holy Spirit, as it was in the beginning, is now, and ever shall be, world without end. Amen!

Chapter Three
Third Station

Jesus Falls for the First Time

Isaiah 53:5

V. We adore thee, O Christ, and praise thee.
R. *Because by thy holy cross, thou hast redeemed the world.*

Meditation
The enemies of your life (Eph. 6:12) who may have caused your downfall now also seek that you never get up from it; but Jesus, in carrying His cross, wearied by its weight and the burden of the sin of man particularly your sins, and the strikes of the soldiers lost His balance and fell beneath it. However, he did not stay down, for the power of God raised Him up to continue His journey to Calvary. Therefore, that same power shall raise you up from your present fall to continue your journey to your destiny and mission on earth.

Prayer

Lord Jesus, thank you for being my perfect example (Heb. 4:15). You always show me the way (John 14:6). Now, Lord, strengthen me in my present fall that I may appropriate your power to rise up again to the shame of my enemies and to your honour and glory forever. Amen!

You satanic and occult spirits (Rev. 12:12, 10: 1-6, 13:1-8, 29:1-6; Ezek. 29:6; Isa. 27:1; Mark 5:1-13) dominions, authorities, powers, false altars (1 Cor. 10:20), shrines, temples and your human agents (Eph. 6:12), after causing my fall, you also now seek that I never get up from it. But you lie! For when my perfect example Jesus fell on His journey to Calvary, the power of our God raised Him up and He was able to rise and still fulfill His destiny – the redemption of man (Acts 2:36).

Therefore, in the name of Jesus and in the authority of His cross and this third station, I decree by fire, by force that the same power shall propel me to rise from my present fall and I shall fulfil my God given destiny. And there is nothing you or anyone else can ever do to stop me (Job 22:28; Matt. 18:18; Heb. 4:16). Amen!

Our Father, who art in heaven, hallowed be thy name. Thy kingdom come, thy will be done on earth, as it is in Heaven. And give us this day our daily bread, and forgive us our trespasses as we forgive those who trespass against us. And lead us not into temptation, but deliver us from evil. Amen!

Hail Mary, full of grace, the Lord is with thee. Blessed art thou among women and blessed is the Fruit of thy womb, Jesus. Holy Mary, Mother of God, pray for us sinners, now and at the hour of our death. Amen!

Glory be to the Father, and to the Son, and to the Holy Spirit, as it was in the beginning, is now, and ever shall be, world without end. Amen!

Chapter Four

Fourth Station
Jesus Beholds His Holy Mother

John 19:25-27

V. We adore thee, O Christ, and praise thee.
R. *Because by thy holy cross, thou hast redeemed the world.*

Meditation
Let your soul, spirit, heart and mind deeply meditate on Jesus seeing His dearly beloved Mother Mary closely in the crowd of people around Him as He journeyed to Calvary and especially when He looked down His cross and saw Mary there beholding Him. Imagine the mutual pain they both shared, fulfilling the prophecy of Simeon to Mary: "And sorrow, like sharp sword, will break your own heart" (Luke 2:35).

Prayer

O my sorrowful Jesus, kindly permit me to share with thee and thy dearest mother the pain thou both didst experience at these encounters. May it, Lord, gain grace for me for a devoted love for your holy mother. Amen!

And you, my dearest mother (John 19:26-27; Rev. 12:17), may my sharing in the meditation of this your meeting with your dear son and my Lord, attract for me your motherly intercession (John 2:1-11), from my Redeemer and Saviour for an outpouring of His mercy and favour upon my life in these my battles against the enemies of my progress and destiny. Amen!

Our Father, who art in heaven, hallowed be thy name. Thy kingdom come, thy will be done on earth, as it is in heaven. And give us this day our daily bread, and forgive us our trespasses as we forgive those who trespass against us. And lead us not into temptation, but deliver us from evil. Amen!

Hail Mary, full of grace, the Lord is with thee. Blessed art thou among women and blessed is the Fruit of thy womb, Jesus. Holy Mary, Mother of God, pray for us sinners, now and at the hour of our death. Amen!

Glory be to the Father, and to the Son, and to the Holy Spirit, as it was in the beginning, is now, and ever shall be, world without end. Amen!

Chapter Five

Fifth Station
Simon Helps Jesus Carry His Cross

Matthew 27:32; Mark 15:21; Luke 23:26

V. We adore thee, O Christ, and praise thee.
R. *Because by thy holy cross, thou hast redeemed the world.*

Meditation
The enemies of your life (Eph. 6:12) often physically and spiritually block your divine helpers from reaching you (Dan. 10:12-13) in order to ensure you never get any sustainable assistance that may enable you to overcome your overwhelming difficulties.

But in this station, Jesus received help from Simon of Cyrene (Matt. 27:32; Mark 15:21; Luke 23:26), enabling Him to rest awhile from the burden of His cross. This strengthened Him to continue His journey to Calvary, fulfilling His mission and destiny (John 19:30, 20:1-17). So it shall be for you.

My dearest, God has provided you with divine helpers in the challenges of your life, but the enemies of your progress and destiny are dispelling them (Dan. 10:11–14). The onus is upon you to cry out like one about to be drowned like Peter (Matt. 14:30) to the Lord of Host, who in His infinite wisdom, knowledge, and power can tear down any obstacle blocking your God appointed divine helpers from reaching out to you to pull you out from your pit of afflictions. My beloved, cry a cry of faith for our loving God is there, awaiting your exercise of trust in Him.

Prayer

O Lord Jesus, my Saviour and Master! At the darkest hour of your journey to Calvary, when it was feared you may never make it there, your executioners, determined at ensuring that you die the shameful death of the cross, constrained Simon of Cyrene to carry your cross. This gave you temporal respite crucial to your fulfilling your mission and destiny (Acts 2:23).

Now, Lord, overwhelming difficulties far beyond my strength have weighted me down and I am deeply sinking in the deep waters with no help in sight. My enemies glare at me in hate and deep resentment, and they fiercely wade off all help from reaching me having intentions that I be choked to death.

So, in my despair, I raise my eyes unto you my Redeemer and Saviour, that, just like you received help from Simon of Cyrene, I may, through thy divine mercy and favour, gain access to the divine helpers you have appointed for my help in this crucial stage of my journey of life. Lord, do not let my enemies gloat over me.

O Jesus my hopes and expectations are completely entrusted in thy promise for my help and rest (Isa. 54:11-17; Matt. 11:28-30; Heb. 3:7-19, 4:1-11). Hence in faith, I decree in the name of Jesus that the eternal sacred power of His cross and this station shall rise as standards against all oppositions of all enemies of my life, progress, and destiny, who are blocking my access to my divine helpers. And by fire and force, I align myself to the access of all my Simons of Cyrene in the name of Jesus Christ. And so I declare that all my godly ordained helpers shall now reach out to help me in the most powerful name of Jesus Christ. (Job 22:28; Matt. 18:18) Amen! Amen! Amen!

Our Father, Who art in heaven, hallowed be thy name. Thy kingdom come, thy will be done on earth, as it is in heaven. And give us this day our daily bread, and forgive us our trespasses as we forgive those who trespass against us. And lead us not into temptation, but deliver us from evil. Amen!

Hail Mary, full of grace, the Lord is with thee. Blessed art thou among women and blessed is the Fruit of thy womb, Jesus. Holy Mary, Mother of God, pray for us sinners, now and at the hour of our death. Amen!

Glory be to the Father, and to the Son, and to the Holy Spirit, as it was in the beginning, is now, and ever shall be, world without end. Amen!

Chapter Six

Sixth Station
Veronica Wipes the Face of Jesus
Isaiah 52:14

V. We adore thee, O Christ, and praise thee.
R. *Because by thy holy cross, thou hast redeemed the world.*

Meditation
Your enemies (Eph. 6:12) who may have taken vows or entered into covenants with demons to ensure you will never get respite from your troubles, but in this station, this courageous woman named Veronica, notwithstanding the danger to her life imposed by the soldiers surrounding Jesus, waded through them to wipe his face. This enabled Him to be refreshed – to breathe and see more clearly from the sweat and blood covering His eyes, thus, strengthening Him to fulfil His mission of salvation.

Dearly beloved, be certain that God in His mercy has provided you with all the Veronicas of your life, but you can only access them through act of faith in Christ Jesus (Eph. 1:1-10). So be courageous like Veronica and invoke the power of God within you to dismantle all obstacles obstructing your Veronicas from reaching out to you so you too, like Jesus, can breathe a breath of fresh air from your numerous troubles.

Prayer

O my most adorable Jesus, one in complete union with the Father, I worship you for you are indeed God! Lord, in your most tormented hour on your way to Calvary, when you were covered in sweat and blood that you could hardly see, this great and courageous woman, Veronica, stepped out to wipe your face notwithstanding the danger to her life, enabling you to be refreshed to fulfil your mission of salvation. I want the same for my life. Amen! So Lord, in thy name, I invoke thy glorious power in thy cross and in this station to attract for me right now, the Veronicas of my life, who shall close their eyes to my faults and be deaf to ugly reports about me but are passionate in their desire for my assistance so I, too, can have relief from my bundles of troubles. Amen!

Now, you enemies of my life (Eph. 6:12), your powers to stop my Veronicas from reaching out to me have been taken away from you by the authority of the cross of Jesus Christ and this sixth station, which all stand as standards against you in perpetuity from any further attempt at obstructing my Veronicas in the name of Jesus Christ. Amen! Amen!

Our Father, who art in heaven, hallowed be thy name. Thy kingdom come, thy will be done on earth, as it is in heaven. And give us this day our daily bread, and forgive us our trespasses as we forgive those who trespass against us. And lead us not into temptation, but deliver us from evil. Amen!

Hail Mary, full of grace, the Lord is with thee. Blessed art thou among women and blessed is the Fruit of thy womb, Jesus. Holy Mary, Mother of God, pray for us sinners, now and at the hour of our death. Amen!

Glory be to the Father, and to the Son, and to the Holy Spirit, as it was in the beginning, is now, and ever shall be, world without end. Amen!

Chapter Seven

Seventh Station
Jesus Falls for the Second Time

Isaiah 53:7

V. We adore thee, O Christ, and praise thee.
R. *Because by thy holy cross, thou hast redeemed the world.*

Meditation

Your enemies laugh at your falling again, your numerous misfortunes resulting in failed businesses and encirclement of debts, troubled relationships, marriage and family crises, security problems, near success syndrome, career crises and so on. And so they ask, "Where is your all-powerful God?" They jeer at you, seeking the evidence of your godliness in your physical success. And seemingly seeing none, they regard you as a failure, one without any more hope.

My dearest, be encouraged and joyful. Do not be dismayed by the taunts of your enemies - the detractors who aim at wearing you down so you may lose focus and possibly abandon your God who is your greatest strength. He is an asset they envy, which you must hold jealously. It is the most valuable of all you have and the most critical to your winning these battles of your life.

Be assured that this lie of the enemy cannot hold water, for indeed, you are not a failure. You are the salt of the earth and the light of the world (Matt. 5:13-14), and your goodness and illumination shall dominate the earth (Matt. 5:i5-1 6).

In carrying His cross, wearied by its weight and the burden of the sin of man, particularly your sins and the strikes of the soldiers, Jesus lost His balance, falling the second time with the cross crushing down over Him (Isa. 53:7). But the power of God raised Him up to continue His mission. And so it shall be for you, if you will be like Peter (Matt. 14:30), who called upon the Lord of Hosts to save you so that your light will illuminate the earth, bringing glory, honour and praise to the Lord (Phil. 2:11). So like an entrapped lamb, shout the name of the Lord for your help. He is standing by and waiting for your cry. Cry now! Cry fiercely!

Prayer

O Jesus! (three times), the Holy Son of God! Light from light, True God from true God, Begotten not made, One in substance with the Father, the Alpha and the Omega, the Great I Am that I Am, the Rock of Ages, the Fountain of my life, my True Joy! I worship and adore you, Lord, and declare that you are truly God!

Now, Lord Jesus, I invoke your Spirit, especially in this seventh station, your second fall and rising on your journey to Calvary, for my rising from every fall of my life and every entanglement that is holding me down. Let the glorious power of your divine presence undo – and break loose every chain, rope, ceiling, web, cage, and key upon my life and destiny. And pull my family and me from any hole in which we may have been caged. I shatter by the force of your name - the Rock of Ages, all obstacles in the path of our fulfilling our destiny. In thy name, Lord, I decree and declare our freedom for ever (Gal. 5: 1; Job 22: 28; Matt. 18:18). Amen!

And you the enemies of my life (Eph. 6:12) by the authority of I Am that I Am, I bar you from coming near me and my family in every form and from all our interests and opportunities. The cross of Jesus and this seventh station will always be standards against all your evil intentions upon our lives (Job 22:28; Matt. 18: 18). Amen!

Our Father, who art in heaven, hallowed be thy name. Thy kingdom come, thy will be done on earth, as it is in heaven. And give us this day our daily bread, and forgive us our trespasses as we forgive those who trespass against us. And lead us not into temptation, but deliver us from evil. Amen!

Hail Mary, full of grace, the Lord is with thee. Blessed art thou among women and blessed is the Fruit of thy womb, Jesus. Holy Mary, Mother of God, pray for us sinners, now and at the hour of our death. Amen!

Glory be to the Father, and to the Son, and to the Holy Spirit, as it was in the beginning, is now, and ever shall be, world without end. Amen!

Chapter Eight

Eighth Station
The Women of Jerusalem Mourn for Jesus

Luke 23:27-31

V. We adore thee, O Christ, and praise thee.
R. *Because by thy holy cross, thou hast redeemed the world.*

Meditation

The enemies of your life (Eph. 6:12) may have caused your failures and ruthlessly encircled you in grave confusion and dirt. They may have made you feel humiliated or believe that your failures have reduced you to nothing, your friends and family have all abandoned you, and you no longer enjoy empathy from anyone. They may have made you believe that you are now without friends and so shall die in frustration and loneliness - a person seemingly forgotten as if dead. You may believe you are no longer consulted on anything even on family and community issues one whose opinion no longer counts. They may make you feel like an imbecile (Ps. 31:11-13).

But here lies the hidden mysterious wisdom and power of our God who thrives in nothingness. The strength of His power is made more manifest in extremely hopeless and most difficult situations when all hope is lost. He works to show the supremacy of His might and power (Exod. 14:13-14) often demonstrated through His mercy and love. And dearest, this is the wisdom of our God, the Faithful One (Rev. 19:11).

This is why, on this eighth station, when Jesus had been abandoned by His friends the apostles and disciples, and suffered rejection and denial and was beaten, wounded and traumatised and seemingly alone, God showed His care and love for Him by raising from among the same people who shouted "Crucify Him! Crucify Him!" a people to show Him compassion which opened up His spirit. And He said, "Women of Jerusalem, do not cry for me but for yourselves and your children..."(Luke 23:20, 28), thus foretelling what would befall Jerusalem as the result of un-repentance, hence calling us to repentance.

Dearest, like these women of Jerusalem who wept in sympathy towards Jesus, raise your deep cry of agony of rejections, denials, and taunts by family, neighbours, friends and associates on high to heaven unto God so He may be moved in compassion to pour down His mercy and love unto you by raising a people to share your pains and your joys with you, thus reversing the intentions of your enemies.

Prayer

My beloved Jesus, when you walked down the road to Calvary, seemingly alone and having been rejected, denied, beaten, wounded, spat upon, and traumatised, God, in His compassion, raised for you a people from among those who had rejected you to show you empathy, which comforted your spirit (Luke 23:27-31).

Now, Lord, may my faith, wailings, tears, and agony of the pains of my rejections, denials, resentments, hatreds, failures, confusions, and humiliations rise up to you as sacrificial offerings, coated in the sweet smelling incense of your blood to win for me your love, mercy, and favour to reverse the wicked intentions of my enemies for my eternal frustration and loneliness, thus, drawing for me a people among my very own brethren, who shall show me compassion, sharing my pains and joys. In all circumstances of my life, I shall never be left without friends – true friends – a people who will always love and cherish me in the name of Jesus Christ. Amen! Amen! Amen!

And you, enemies of my life (Eph. 6:12), the cross of Jesus and this station shall remain forever standards against you, having reversed your wicked intentions for me in the name of Jesus Christ. Amen!

Our Father, who art in heaven, hallowed be thy name. Thy kingdom come, thy will be done on earth, as it is in heaven. And give us this day our daily bread, and forgive us our trespasses as we forgive those who trespass against us. And lead us not into temptation, but deliver us from evil. Amen!

Hail Mary, full of grace, the Lord is with thee. Blessed art thou among women and blessed is the Fruit of thy womb, Jesus. Holy Mary, Mother of God, pray for us sinners, now and at the hour of our death. Amen!

Glory be to the Father, and to the Son, and to the Holy Spirit, as it was in the beginning, is now, and ever shall be, world without end. Amen!

Chapter Nine

Ninth Station
Jesus Falls for the Third Time
Isaiah 53:7,8

V. We adore thee, O Christ, and praise thee.
R. *Because by thy holy cross, thou hast redeemed the world.*

Meditation
The enemies of your life (Eph. 6:12) having encircled you in seemingly insurmountable confusion, pressure, and burden, which cause you inevitable repeated falls, and now seeing how pitiable you are, believe you are finished. They think that your situation is hopeless so they can also spit and possibly urinate on you. But this is a lie from the pit of hell, for with God nothing is impossible (Luke 1:37). You belong to God for you are His sacred possessions. And He defends and protects you against all who hurt you (Jer. 2:3).

Therefore, be strengthened while holding unto God, resisting the enemy even with the last strength still in you (James 4:7), for in that instant God's power is released to augment your strength, bringing awesome transformation, just like it was for Jesus. Even though he fell the third time, He was strengthened to rise from the fall and still fulfilled His destiny (Isa. 53:11; Act 2:23; Heb. 6:13-20). You shall fulfil your destiny! It is the will of God for your life as the salt and light of the world (Matt. 5:13-16). You must resist any power from taking it away from you (James 4:7).

So like the disciples, with the last strength in you, shout to the Lord "Master, Master! I am about to die (Luke 8:24)!" And then, experience the moment of change of your life to confound your enemies (Dan. 3:16-30).

Prayer

My loving Jesus, how great thou art! What an awesome God you are! You are a marvel! No one, Lord, is like you! Your works showcase your wisdom and your power. Your authority surmounts the mountains, oceans, and seas. And your Word can never be changed. You are a joy to know!

And so, Lord, in confidence of your faithfulness to your covenants, I call to you " Master, Master! Do not let me die (Luke 8:24)!" Do not allow my enemies to gloat over me for I belong to you (Jer. 2:3). Rise in your power, O God, and save me, for my enemies are more powerful than I am. Though I am weak, they strike me without mercy. I am helpless O Lord, without you. In my union with you, we have become one (Rom. 6:3-5; John 14:23), so you are my power. Therefore, right now, I call forth the power I share with you – thy glorious, mysterious power in thy cross and in this ninth station to my defense against my enemies who are strangling me to death. In thy name, Lord, I decree and declare, that I am free! (Col. 2: 8-15; Mark 16:16- 18; Job 22:28; Matt. 18:18) Amen!

And now, you enemies of my life (Eph. 6:12), you strike me in my helplessness? You erroneously think I am finished? Can't you see that I am an indwelling of God? That the Trinity abides in me? (John 14:23). I raise God's Word in Jeremiah. 2:3 against you, for the Lord says He will defend and protect me against all my enemies, - all who hurt me. And I also invoke the cross of Jesus and this ninth station to prevail against you in perpetuity because, in this station, though Jesus fell the third time, the power of God enabled Him to rise up and thus fulfill His destiny.

So, I rise from this fall in that same power and decree that I shall fulfil my God given destiny (Job 22:28; Matt. 18:18; 2Cor. 5:20). In the name of Jesus, His cross, and this station shall be my defence and my protection as His descendant from any further fall from you in my life (Isa. 53:10). Amen!

Our Father, who art in heaven, hallowed be thy name. Thy kingdom come, thy will be done on earth, as it is in heaven. And give us this day our daily bread, and forgive us our trespasses as we forgive those who trespass against us. And lead us not into temptation, but deliver us from evil. Amen!

Hail Mary, full of grace, the Lord is with thee. Blessed art thou among women and blessed is the Fruit of thy womb, Jesus. Holy Mary, Mother of God, pray for us sinners, now and at the hour of our death. Amen!

Glory be to the Father, and to the Son, and to the Holy Spirit, as it was in the beginning, is now, and ever shall be, world without end. Amen!

Chapter Ten

Tenth Station
Jesus is Stripped of His Garments

Matthew 27:35; Mark 15:24; Luke 23:34; John 19:23-24

V. We adore thee, O Christ, and praise thee.
R. *Because by thy holy cross, thou hast redeemed the world.*

Meditation

The enemies of your life (Eph. 6:12), though they may have caused your troubles and sufferings, are yet not satisfied. So they are further seeking your final humiliation. But then, in your union with Christ Jesus, He has in this station, fully satisfied this demand, having suffered humiliation in being stripped of His garments (John 19:23—24). Since He, your ransom, has paid the price of your humiliation, you have been completely set free from any further dishonour to your life (Gal. 5:1). Therefore, be confident in the assurance that you cannot be humiliated again, for the Spirit and power of God is in you and shall workout a safety-net for you in this your present problems (1 John 2:24, 3:19-23,5:1-5; 1 (Cor. 10:12-13).

Prayer

Lord Jesus, you are a dependable God and faithful to your covenant! No god is as thoughtful as you are. Your love and care for me are immeasurable. Thank you, Lord, for covering my nakedness and shielding me from the humiliations of my life through thy cross and this tenth station, thus thwarting the plots of the enemies of my destiny.

You have changed my status of shame and dishonor to honour and integrity, thereby giving me a song of praise, worship, and adoration to you, my God. It is unheard of, Lord, that anyone can undo what you have done, closing a door you have opened or opening one you have closed (Rev. 3:7). My enemies boast in their god and their power. And having laid new siege for a final onslaught for my humiliation, they now taunt me. So, Lord Jesus, in faithfulness to your Word, which you watch to see come to pass (Jer. 1:12), and in this station, sustain my victory. Keep me safe from defeat and humiliation so my enemies will not gloat over me. Thank you, Lord, for I know you have answered my prayers (Matt. 11:29; John 14:13-14). Amen!

You lying, creeping, and deceptive spirits, you are not satisfied with the troubles you have caused me but also seek further my humiliation. Well, you shall be disappointed. The Lord, my ransom (Isa. 53:4-7), paid that debt in this station, having been stripped in disgrace (John 19:23–24). So this further demand is thus nullified, as it cannot legally be paid twice. Therefore, I invoke the cross of Jesus and this station as standards against you for my further humiliation forever. Amen!

Our Father, who art in heaven, hallowed be thy name. Thy kingdom come, thy will be done on earth, as it is in heaven. And give us this day our daily bread, and forgive us our trespasses as we forgive those who trespass against us. And lead us not into temptation, but deliver us from evil. Amen!

Hail Mary, full of grace, the Lord is with thee. Blessed art thou among women and blessed is the Fruit of thy womb, Jesus. Holy Mary, Mother of God, pray for us sinners, now and at the hour of our death. Amen!

Glory be to the Father, and to the Son, and to the Holy Spirit, as it was in the beginning, is now, and ever shall be, world without end. Amen!

Chapter Eleven

Eleventh Station

Jesus is Nailed to the Cross

Matthew 27:35; Mark 15:14; Luke23:33; John 19:18

V. We adore thee, O Christ, and praise thee.
R. *Because by thy holy cross, thou hast redeemed the world.*

Meditation

The enemies of your life, even though they may have caused you excruciating sorrow and suffering, dishonor, and defeat, still demand that you be crushed completely, squeezed to death. That's what Jesus, the Lord of Hosts, suffered while being nailed to the cross. His executioners so much wanted with great passion that He be crucified on the cross before His death. It was everything to them, so they conscripted Simon of Cyrene to help Him carry the cross, ensuring he got to Calvary for crucifixion.

In the same way, though, you may have been punished for your offences. You may have been wounded, humiliated, hated, resented, rejected and isolated. Yet, your enemies are still unsatisfied and further seek for you to be crushed. Why? Because of who you are - a child of the living God. Do know, my dear, that the world hates all children of God. God promised you that. Why? It is very simple! Your ways, attitudes, beliefs, convictions, and actions will always be in conflict with ways of the world, leading to misunderstandings and conflicts, just as God's truths are in conflict with the world's. So when you act in consonance with your convictions based on God's truth, you raise hell around you

(John 15:18-25). In this, some have been stoned (Acts 7:54 -59), so you are not alone (John 15:18-21).

However, be assured that victory is yours, for Jesus has overcome the world (John 16:33), and your faith in Him guarantees you victory over the world (1John 5:1-5). When He was nailed to the cross, you were nailed with Him through your baptism. So because you were crushed with Him on the cross, His victory through the cross over the world is then also yours (Rom. 6:3-5).

So be joyful, for your victory is certain. In addition, the crushing-push of your enemies over you is actually your gate pass to victory, for it activates God's defence over you because He abhors oppression over the weak especially the defenceless (Ps. 34:1-6, 18, 35:10). So do not worry. Trust in His covenant promise and faithfulness for your defence and protection from the enemies of your life (Jer. 2:3).

Prayer

What can I say, Lord, but thank you! Yes, Lord, thank you for your victory over the world (John 16:33), which guarantees mine (1John 5:1-5). When those nails pierced through your hands and your feet, spreading out excruciating shock waves of pain through you, blood spurted. The blood then sealed God's new covenant with man. The enemy had been tricked. The shedding of your blood and your death brought the cleansing redemption upon man, restoring him to his original position with God, a mystery beyond the understanding of the enemy (Isa. 53:8, 10; Zech. 13:1; Col. 1:19-20). This is why, Lord, you are the Fountain of knowledge. You are indeed wisdom - the all-knowing God. It is a great privilege and honour for me to know you and to be counted as your sacred possession (Jer. 2:3). I will forever worship, adore and glorify you, my most loving God. Amen!

And, now, you, my enemies (Eph. 6:12), your war games for my being crushed have collapsed. Jesus has gained victory over you (John 16:33). When He was nailed to the cross, He became a curse, crushed to the bones. And in my baptism, I am one with Him. The price of His curse was for my freedom, being my ransom. His blood has paid this price. Therefore, I cannot be crushed (Rom. 6:3-4).

Hence I raise the cross of Jesus and this eleventh station as perpetual standards against you from any further attempt at my being crushed in the name of Jesus Christ. Amen!

Our Father, who art in heaven, hallowed be thy name. Thy kingdom come, thy will be done on earth, as it is in heaven. And give us this day our daily bread, and forgive us our trespasses as we forgive those who trespass against us. And lead us not into temptation, but deliver us from evil. Amen!

Hail Mary, full of grace, the Lord is with thee. Blessed art thou among women and blessed is the Fruit of thy womb, Jesus. Holy Mary, Mother of God, pray for us sinners, now and at the hour of our death. Amen!

Glory be to the Father, and to the Son, and to the Holy Spirit, as it was in the beginning, is now, and ever shall be, world without end. Amen!

Chapter Twelve

Twelfth Station
Jesus Dies on the Cross

Isaiah 53:6, 10; Zechariah 12:10; Matthew 27:50; Mark15:37; Luke 23:46; John 19:30; Philippians 2:8-9

V. We adore thee, O Christ, and praise thee.
R. *Because by thy holy cross, thou hast redeemed the world.*

Meditation
After the shedding of His blood on the cross and through the journey to Calvary, Jesus knew His mission of redemption had been accomplished. Though in great pain and agony, yet out of love and care, He was still able to ensure the welfare of His mother and the disciple He loved most, by intimately connecting them, thus entrusting the church to the love and care of His mother (John 19:26-27). Then, He took a drink to fulfil the remaining word of the prophet and thereafter declared "It is finished" (John 19:30). This means that every facet of the law, psalms and the prophets has been fulfilled. He has accomplished His Father's will – restoration of man's affinity with God (Col. 1:19-20). He then bowed His head and died (John 19:30). His death was the confirmation of the fulfilment of His mission and destiny (Isa. 53:10-12; Acts. 2:23).

Therefore, my dearest, you are one with God. It is your free gift and right in the kingdom (Jer. 2:3; 1 John 5:20; 1 John 3:1-3). Let no power take away this truth from you. At His death, the Lord has poured out His Spirit in you, and you live in complete union with Him (John 19:30; 1 John 2:27). This union avails you the totality of His being – His divinity, knowledge and wisdom, perfect understanding, glory, honour, authority and power, and so on (1 John 3:9).

So, rise in the spirit, and in confidence of who you are and confront the enemies who seek your life and death. They can neither take your life nor destroy anything that belongs to you, including your interests and opportunities for they are not in their hands, but in God's. Therefore, purify yourself. And like the Great Lion of Judea, your Master, bark and bite, for the Lord said, "The kingdom of God suffers violence, but the violent, take it by force" (Matt. 11:12).

Prayer

O Jesus, my Lord, the beloved of and the glory of the Father, thank you for loving me and, sacrificing your life that I may live. Through your death, you have redeemed me from all my guilts and condemnations, thus guaranteeing a new life for me. You, Lord, are the fount of love and epitome of righteousness. You gave me your life, making me fulfilled, restoring my life back. You have filled me in your awesome power, enriching me in the treasures of your wisdom and authority. Now, I have become a blazing fire, and a terror to our enemies, all to your honour and glory. So I match out in this battle against our enemies and in thy name, Lord summon the battalion of angels of heaven led by arch angels Michael and Uriel to match out with me. Amen!

And now, you, the enemies of my God, and my life, you feel you have the final say to my future and destiny, to make and unmake, because the Lord allowed you to torment me in order to use it to draw me back to Himself? Well, I have gone back to my root, and the power of the kingdom of my Father now surrounds me, I am untouchable, far beyond you (Num. 23:21-24).

Therefore, I rain down the blood of the Lamb on your kingdom, uprooting it from its foundation, smashing all its pillars and pulling down all altars, encircling all in the consuming fire of the Holy Ghost, with the angels guarding every exit without a chance of your escape (Rev. 20:9). The game is up. You have lost the battle over me (Gal. 5:1). I told you I'm untouchable (Num. 23:21-24), the apple of the Lord's eye (Zach. 2:8), His sacred possession (Jer. 2:3).

Now, in the name of Jesus Christ, let the mighty angels of the Lord chain and bind you up, and then drag you into the dungeon where you truly belong and where you shall remain until the day of the Lord, when you shall be judged (Rev. 20:10). The cross of Jesus and this station shall forever be standards against you from ever causing any more death in my life in any form (Job 22:28). Amen!

In the power of the name of Jesus, I give back life to everything that is dead in me and restore everything that has ever been taken away from me and all that the devourers and cankerworms have eaten (Joel 2:25). I decree and declare life to all my interests and opportunities and affirm I shall fulfil my mission and destiny on earth to the glory of God the Father (2 Cor. 5:20; Job 22:28; Matt. 18:18). Amen! In the name of my Master and Lord Jesus, I also decree and declare that it is finished. I shall overcome, for the good Lord, through his death on the cross, has won for me my battles with you, my enemies, so I may enjoy fullness of life in God (Col. 2:11-15; Rev. 1:16-20, 19:15, 20-21, 20:9-10; John 10:10). Amen! Amen! Amen!

Our Father, who art in heaven, hallowed be thy name. Thy kingdom come, thy will be done on earth, as it is in heaven. And give us this day our daily bread, and forgive us our trespasses as we forgive those who trespass against us. And lead us not into temptation, but deliver us from evil. Amen!

Hail Mary, full of grace, the Lord is with thee. Blessed art thou among women and blessed is the Fruit of thy womb, Jesus. Holy Mary, Mother of God, pray for us sinners, now and at the hour of our death. Amen!

Glory be to the Father, and to the Son, and to the Holy Spirit, as it was in the beginning, is now, and ever shall be, world without end. Amen!

Chapter Thirteen

Thirteenth Station
Jesus Is Taken Down from the Cross

Mark 15:46; Luke 23:50-53

V. We adore thee, O Christ, and praise thee.
R. *Because by thy holy cross, thou hast redeemed the world.*

Meditation

Behold the wounded body of Jesus the victim being taken down from the cross (Mark 15:46; Luke 23:53). Imagine the motherly pain and anguish that tore the heart of Mary in that instance of beholding the lifeless body of her dearly beloved son, but she was surely consoled by the full knowledge that He had lived in full obedience to the Father's will, fulfilling His mission (Acts 2:23; Isa. 53:10-12). Mary could also easily perceive feeling fully fulfilled herself, having excellently accomplished her own mission and destiny of being the mother of the Messiah–the sufferer (Isa. 53:10-12; Luke 1:26-38; Acts17:3; Matt. 16:16, 21; Acts 18:28).

You can also easily imagine the celebration in the kingdom of darkness, who in illusion believed that God's purpose and will for man's redemption had been quashed with the death of the Messiah, without really knowing that God had tricked it. Yes, the Messiah will die, but the path to His death, the cross will shed His blood needed for God's purposed redemption. The enemy had believed that His death would stop the mission, but God had purposed it to be its fulfilment (1Pet. 1:18 -19; 1John 5:6). This mysterious wisdom was beyond the comprehension of Satan, confirming God's supremacy of wisdom.

In the same way, the enemy believes that by entangling you in untold difficulties, you will most likely denounce God, but the reverse is the case (Job 2:3-6). The mysterious power in your baptism is actually greatly activated in hopelessness if you could, with the last breath in you, invoke the power of God within you to set off a surge of God's divine mercy to your help (Ps. 34:1-6, 18, 35:10, 145:13-14). This confounds the enemy and is part of the secret treasures in the inheritance of the kingdom of God (Col. 1:11-12; Eph. 1:3-4).

Dearest, know yea that when Jesus was taken down from the cross, your afflictions were indeed taken down with Him because you were crucified with Him through your baptism. His body bore the marks, the evidence of your afflictions. So you cannot remain afflicted, having been freed from the afflictions of your life by Christ (Rom. 6:3-4). Therefore, just point to the defeated enemy the afflicted body of Jesus as the price of your afflictions and your freedom (Col. 2:12-15).

However, there is a caveat. Your obedience to God's command is your access pass to the treasure as the proof of your faith and sonship. So raise your access pass and push the door wide open, for it guarantees you automatic access (1 John 5:1-5). If you have challenge with the pass due to sin, you reconcile with God, and once again declare your pass (1 John1:8-10).

Prayer

Lord Jesus, what an awesome thoughtful God you are! Even before time began, God had purposed all things (Eph. 1:9-11; 2Tim. 1:9) that you shall be born of a virgin through the power of the Holy Spirit to establish His kingdom on earth (Luke 1:26-38), you shall suffer and be killed by men by being crucified on the cross, man gains redemption from sin through your death and be restored in affinity with God; you shall rise from death on the third day and be enthroned in everlasting kingship. These you have righteously fulfilled (Luke 1:26-38; John 2:1-7 Isa53:10-12;Acts 2:22- 36; Rev. 5:6-14). Through your suffering, you have gained for me freedom from the world and given me a life of joy, knowing you the only true God (John 17:1-3; 1 John 5:1-5, 13-15, 20). What else, Lord, can I ever ask for? I will forever celebrate you, my King, and show the world how loving and merciful you are. You are worthy of my praise, worship, and adoration. Amen!

And as Jesus was taken down from the cross, so have my afflictions been taken away from me. Therefore, you cannot afflict me afresh, for Jesus, through His death, has gained for me victory over you (John16:33; Rom. 3:25). I have appropriated His righteousness; hence, the life I live now is not mine, but His (Col. 3:3-4), for He dwelleth in me (Col. 1:27; Gal. 2:20). My faith in Him gains for me the grace to live in obedience to His commands (Rom. 1:17) and I confess my sins daily unto him and His blood atones all my unrighteousness (1John 1:8-10). So you have nothing to hold against me. You have lost your power over me (Gal. 5:1). Hence, in the name of Jesus, His cross and this station shall remain forever standards against you from any further affliction upon my life (Job 22:28; Matt. 18:18). Amen!

Our Father, who art in heaven, hallowed be thy name. Thy kingdom come, thy will be done on earth, as it is in heaven. And give us this day our daily bread, and forgive us our trespasses as we forgive those who trespass against us. And lead us not into temptation, but deliver us from evil. Amen!

Hail Mary, full of grace, the Lord is with thee. Blessed art thou among women and blessed is the Fruit of thy womb, Jesus. Holy Mary, Mother of God, pray for us sinners, now and at the hour of our death. Amen!

Glory be to the Father, and to the Son, and to the Holy Spirit, as it was in the beginning, is now, and ever shall be, world without end. Amen!

Chapter Fourteen

Fourteenth Station
Jesus Is Laid in the Tomb

Matthew 27:57-61; Mark 15:42-47; Luke 23:50-56; John 19:38-42

V. We adore thee, O Christ, and praise thee.
R. *Because by thy holy cross, thou hast redeemed the world.*

Meditation

After being taken down from the cross, Jesus's body was wrapped in linen sheet with the spices according to Jewish custom of preparing a body for burial and placed in the newly dug tomb. Then a large stone was rolled across the entrance to the tomb (Matt. 27:57-61; Mark 15:42-47; Luke 23:50-56; John 19:38-42).

Dearest, know for certain that the afflictions of your life, your old self were, indeed at your baptism, buried with Jesus in that tomb. And with the stone on the entrance, they were sealed from ever re-emerging in your life (Rom. 6:3-4). That stone, the rock, is Christ (Exod. 17:5-6; 1Cor. 10:1-4). Though buried, it still stands at the entrance as the guard and guarantee of your freedom, bringing His words "It is finished" into reality (John19:30). It is the unending mystery of our God. And it is marvellous in our eyes.

The only thing that brings afflictions back into your life is sin. Of course, you can deal with this, for no child of God continues to sin. God's grace abounds to deal with that, especially if one is disposed to it. These are the treasures of our kingdom. (1John 3:9; 1 John 5:18).

So repent of your sins and genuinely, as a demonstration of your radical faith in God commit to a new life of radical obedience to God's commands for the rest of your days.

Prayer

O my sweet Jesus, thank you for securing my life and showing me the path to true life, your cross. You have given me the best gift of my life, eternal life (John 5:21, 10:28). Now, I can live life to its fullness (John 10:10). Though you lay buried to rest from your conquest, you were still mysteriously at work for the ancient brothers who have been awaiting your arrival since the beginning of time (Matt. 27:51-53; 1Peter 3:19-20).

Lord, I promise you from henceforth to always do your will, to live the gospel, and to be a model of your glory on earth. This is my little way of showing you my gratitude for granting me rest from all the traumas of my life, for I know for certain that my prayers have been answered (1 John 5:13-15). Amen!

As for you, I have nothing more to say to you, for Jesus, my conqueror, has not only defeated you but made a public spectacle of you, having crowned me in glory for all to behold (Col. 2:11-15; Phil. 2:15). So be sure of one thing, I will forever remain your enemy and will be a tormenting instrument in the hand of God against your kingdom. Our paths will never cross ever again for the power of my God now abides in me forever. Amen!

Our Father, who art in heaven, hallowed be thy name. Thy kingdom come, thy will be done on earth, as it is in heaven. And give us this day our daily bread, and forgive us our trespasses as we forgive those who trespass against us. And lead us not into temptation, but deliver us from evil. Amen!

Hail Mary, full of grace, the Lord is with thee. Blessed art thou among women and blessed is the Fruit of thy womb, Jesus. Holy Mary, Mother of God, pray for us sinners, now and at the hour of our death. Amen!

Glory be to the Father, and to the Son, and to the Holy Spirit, as it was in the beginning, is now, and ever shall be, world without end. Amen!

Conclusion

Intentions of the Holy Father the Pope

Our Father, who art in heaven, hallowed be thy name. Thy kingdom come, thy will be done on earth, as it is in heaven. And give us this day our daily bread and forgive us our trespasses as we forgive those who trespass against us. And lead us not into temptation, but deliver us from evil. Amen!

Hail Mary, full of grace, the Lord is with thee. Blessed art thou among women and blessed is the Fruit of thy womb, Jesus. Holy Mary, Mother of God, pray for us sinners, now and at the hour of our death. Amen!

Glory be to the Father, and to the Son, and to the Holy Spirit, as it was in the beginning, is now, and ever shall be, world without end. Amen

Closing Prayer

O Lord, the Holy Spirit of Jesus, thank you for the out pouring of your divine presence and grace, which enabled me to fully share in this journey of the passion of Jesus on the cross.

Now, my hopes and expectations are entrusted in the miraculous eternal glorious resurrection power of our God who raised you up from death on the third day, freeing you from its captivity into the immortal glorious life of the father where you are now seated in eternal rulership and reignship with Him (Matt. 28: 5-7; Mark 16:6-7; Luke 24:5-7; 1Cor. 15: 3-4, 51-57; Rev. 5: 6-14).

This hope through my union with you that having shared in your death, I also share in the resurrection power and have been raised up with you to rule with you in the heavenly world (Rom. 6:3-11; Eph. 2: 6) far above all ruling spirits of the universe (Col. 2:20), and in your covenant, the promise that my hopes shall not be dashed (Rom. 10:11), makes my joy complete. I will forever rejoice in your presence, and may it please you, Lord, that this moment for me never ends. Amen!

www.ingramcontent.com/pod-product-compliance
Lightning Source LLC
Chambersburg PA
CBHW041524090426
42737CB00038B/112